A COLLECTION OF ESSAYS

By

THOMAS LOVE PEACOCK

British Library Cataloguing-in-Publication Data
A catalogue record for this book is available
from the British Library

CONTENTS

THOMAS LOVE PEACOCK 5

THE SATIRISTS AND FANTASTICS 8

THE FOUR AGES OF POETRY. 13

RECOLLECTIONS OF CHILDHOOD 30

THE LAST DAY OF WINDSOR FOREST 36

PROSPECTUS: CLASSICAL EDUCATION 45

THOMAS LOVE PEACOCK

By Sir Walter Raleigh
from
On Writers and Writing

THERE is nothing misanthropical about Peacock. He admires, and loves. All that is simple and matter of affection, and private, is dear to him. He laughs at idealists, and makers of systems. Yet---here is the strange thing---he is not common sense against the idea. He has, deep down in him, a great love for ideas. How easy to make fun of Rousseau, Mme de Genlis, Thomas Day--- all that world of theory which belongs to the French Revolution! Peacock does make fun of it, but he has been touched by it. The two most virtuous characters in *Melincourt* are Sir Oran Haut-ton and Sylvan Forester---separate embodiments of the natural man of the revolutionary philosophy. Life in the woods---life in a cottage with a garden---Peacock is almost passionate about these. Yet he praises them chiefly in conversations that take place round tables amply suppled with old silver and madeira.

He was a friend of Shelley, and a wine-drinker---perhaps that best describes him. His friendship for Shelley had in it some kinship of ideas, not a merely personal liking. Indeed, Peacock himself was something of a theorist. He loved the consistency of the Latin mind; he adored logic; he loved a rebel, if the rebel was in earnest, as Shelley was. His ridicule of the other poets of the time turns for the most part on a single point, that they have given up their youthful creeds and have settled down in comfort.

Talk gives the structure of his books. They are a world of

talk. "It's all very fine talking," people say, "but is it practical?" In Peacock the standard is reversed. "It's all very practical, but is it fine talking?" The atmosphere of conviviality in the novels keeps the differences from bursting into drama. When the dispute waxes hot someone says, "Buz the bottle."

Allow for the difference between a persecuted preacher of the gospel and a prosperous clerk in the Examiner's office of the East India Company, and Peacock's work is a kindly *Pilgrim's Progress.* He gives his characters the same kind of names. Bunyan would have said it was a Pilgrm's Progress by Mr Byends of the City of Fairspeech.

Type in Peacock hardly ever passes into character. His work continually borders on character drawing, but he values the play of wit and theory too well. The whole world is a *salon* to him.

If there are any of Peacock's persons who are felt to be living human characters, they are to be found among his young ladies and his drunkards. The first are real, perhaps because they are pleasant and sensible (which few of the men are), perhaps because the author takes fewer freedoms in the portraiture. It is difficult to say exactly how they make so pleasant an impression---probably by their freedom from censoriousness, and by the good will of the other characters towards them. A novelist may learn something from the wisdom of Lord Halifax in his *Advice to a Daughter:*

"The triumph of wit is to make your good nature subdue your censure, to be quick in seeing fults and slow in exposing them. You are to consider that the invisible thing called a *Good Name* is made up of the breth of numbers that speak well of you; so that if by a disobliging word you silence the meanest, the gale will be less strong which is to bear up your esteem. And though nothing is so vain as the eager pursuit of empty applause, yet to be well thought of and to be kindly used by the world is like a glory about a woman's head' 'tis a perfumeshe carrieth about with her and leaveth wherever she goeth; 'tis a charm against ill-will. Malice may empty her quiver, but cannot wound; the dirt will not stick, the jests will not take."

Something of this charm is to be found in Peacock's heroines, so to call them.

George Meredith was Peacock's son-in-law, and learned more from Peacock than from any other writer; in his characters of women especially, and his convivial scenes.

There is, it has often been remarked a certain Gallic quality in Peacock's wit. It is gay and polished, and usually subtle. Our satirists are commonly heavy-weight prize-fighters. Our irony is often as strong as cheese. He has the spirit of wise mischief, like M. Anatole France.

---from *On Writing and Writers* by Walter Raleigh, being extracts from his note-books, selected and edited by George Gordon, London. (1926), pp. 151-54.

THE SATIRISTS
AND FANTASTICS

By Virginia Woolf
from
"Phases of Fiction" in *Granite and Rainbow*

THE CONFUSED feelings which the psychologists have roused in us, the extraordinary intricacy which they have revealed to us, the network of fine and scarcely intelligible yet profoundly interesting emotions in which they have involved us, set up a craving for relief, at first so primitive that it is almost a physical sensation. The mind feels like a sponge saturated full with sympathy and understanding; it needs to dry itself, to contract upon something hard. Satire and the sense that the satirist gives us that he has the world well within his grasp, so that it is at the mercy of his pen, precisely fulfil our needs.

A further instinct will lead us to pass over such famous satirists as Voltaire and Anatole France in favour of someone writing in our own tongue, writing English. For without any disrespect to the translator we have grown intolerably weary in reading Dostoevsky, as if we were reading with the wrong spectacles or as if a mist had formed between us and the page. We come to feel that every idea is slipping about in a suit badly cut and many sizes too large for it. For a translation makes us understand more clearly than the lectures of any professor the difference between raw words and written words; the nature and importance of what we call style. Even an inferior writer, using his own tongue upon his own ideas, works a change at once which is agreeable and remarkable. Under his pen the sentence shrinks and wraps itself firmly round the meaning, if it be but a little one. The loose, the baggy, shrivels up. And while a writer of passable English will do this, a writer like Peacock does infinitely more.

When we open *Crotchet Castle* and read that first very long sentence which begins, 'In one of those beautiful valleys, through which the Thames (not yet polluted by the tide, the scouring of cities or even the minor defilement of the sandy streams of Surrey)', it would be difficult to describe the relief it gives us, except metaphorically. First there is the shape which recalls something visually delightful, like a flowing wave or the lash of a whip vigorously flung; then as phrase joins phrase and one parenthesis after another pours in its tributary, we have a sense of the whole swimming stream gliding beneath old walls with the shadows of ancient buildings and the glow of green lawns reflected in it. And what is even more delightful after the immensities and obscurities in which we have been living, we are in a world so manageable in scale that we can take its measure, tease it and ridicule it. It is like stepping out into the garden on a perfect September morning when every shadow is sharp and every colour bright after a night of storm and thunder. Nature has submitted to the direction of man. Man himself is dominated by his intelligence. Instead of being manysided, complicated, elusive, people possess one idiosyncrasy apiece, which crystallizes them into sharp separate characters, colliding briskly when they meet. They seem ridiculously and grotesquely simplified out of all knowledge. Dr. Folliott, Mr. Firedamp, Mr. Skionar, Mr. Chainmail, and the rest seem after the tremendous thickness and bulk of the Guermantes and the Stavrogins nothing but agreeable caricatures which a clever old scholar has cut out of a sheet of black paper with a pair of scissors. But on looking closer we find that though it would be absurd to credit Peacock with any desire or perhaps capacity to explore the depths of the soul, his reticence is not empty but suggestive. The character of Dr. Folliott is drawn in three strokes of the pen. What lies between is left out. But each stroke indicates the mass behind it, so that the reader can make it out for himself; while it has, because of this apparent simplicity, all the sharpness of a caricature. The world so happily constituted that theTe is always trout for breakfast, wine in the cellar, and some amusing contretemps, such as the cook setting herself alight and being put out by the footman, to make us laugh---a world where there is nothing more pressing to do than to 'glide over the face of the waters, discussing everything and settling nothing', is not the world of pure fantasy; -it is close enough to be a parody of our world and to make our own follies and the solemnities of our institutions look a little silly.

The satirist does not, like the psychologist, labour under the oppression of omniscience. He has leisure to play with his mind freely, ironically. His sympathies are not deeply engaged. His sense of humour is not submerged.

But the prime distinction lies in the changed attitude towards reality. In the psychologists the huge burden of facts is based upon a firm foundation of dinner, luncheon, bed and breakfast. It is with surprise, yet with relief and a start of pleasure, that we accept Peacock's version of the world, which ignores so much, simplifies so much, gives the old globe a spin and shows another face of it on the other side. It is unnecessary to be quite so painstaking, it seems. And, after all, is not this quite as real, as true as the other? And perhaps all this posher about 'reality' is overdone. The great gain is perhaps that our relation with things is more distant. We reap the benefit of a more poetic point of view. A line like the charming 'At Godstow, they gathered hazel on the grave of Rosamond' could be written only by a writer who was at a certain distance from his people, so that there need be no explanations. For certainly with Trollope's people explanations would have been necessary; we should have wanted to know what they had been doing, gathering hazel, and where they had gone for dinner afterwards and how the carriage had met them. 'They', however, being Chainmail, Skionar, and the rest, are at liberty to gather hazel on the grave of Rosamond if they like; as they are free to sing a song if it so pleases them or to debate the march of mind.

The romantic took the same liberty but for another purpose. In the satirist we get not a sense of wildness and the soul's adventures, but that the mind is free and therefore sees through and dispenses with much that is taken seriously by writers of another calibre. There are, of course, limitations, reminders, even in the midst of our pleasure, of boundaries that we must not pass. We cannot imagine in the first place that the writer of such exquisite sentences can cover many reams of paper; they cost too much to make. Then again a writer who gives us so keen a sense of his own personality by the shape of his phrase is limited. We are always being brought into touch, not with Peacock himself, as with Trollope himself (for there is no giving away of his own secrets; he does not conjure up the very shape of himself and the sound of his laughter as Trollope does), but all the time our thought is taking the colour of his thought, we are insensibly thinking in his measure. If we write, we try to write in his manner, and this brings us into far greater intimacy,with him than with writers like Trollope again or Scott, who wrap their thought up quite adequately in a duffle grey blanket which wears well and suits everything. This may in the end, of course, lead to some restriction. Style may carry with it, especially in prose, so much personality that it keeps us within the range of that personality. Peacock pervades his book. . . .

---from "The Satirists and Fantastics," a section of the long essay, "Phases of Fiction" in *Granite and Rainbow* Essays by Virginia Woolf, London. (1958), pp. 130-33. The essay originally appeared in *The Bookman* April, May, & June, 1929.

THE FOUR AGES OF POETRY

1820

Qui inter haec nutriuntur non magis sapere possunt,
quam bene olere qui in culina habitant. PETRONIUS. [1]

POETRY, like the world, may be said to have four ages, but in a different order: the first age of poetry being the age of iron; the second, of gold; the third, of silver; and the fourth, of brass.

The first, or iron age of poetry, is that in which rude bards celebrate in rough numbers the exploits of ruder chiefs, in days when every man is a warrior, and when the great practical maxim of every form of society, "to keep what we have and to catch what we can," is not yet disguised under names of justice and forms of law, but is the naked motto of the naked sword, which is the only judge and jury in every question of *meum* and *tuum*.In these days, the only three trades flourishing (besides that of priest which flourishes always) are those of king, thief, and beggar: the beggar being for the most part a king deject, and the thief a king expectant. The first question asked of a stranger is, whether he is a beggar or a thief: [2] the stranger, in reply, usually assumes the first, and awaits a convenient opportunity to prove his claim to the second appellation.

The natural desire of every man to engross to himself as much power and property as he can acquire by any of the means which might makes right, is accompanied by the no less natural desire of making known to as many people as possible the extent to which he has been a winner in this universal game. The

13

successful warrior becomes a chief; the successful chief becomes a king: his next want is an organ to disseminate the fame of his achievements and the extent of his possessions; and this organ he finds in a bard, who is always ready to celebrate the strength of his arm, being first duly inspired by that of his liquor. This is the origin of poetry, which, like all other trades, takes its rise in the demand for the commodity, and flourishes in proportion to the extent of the market.

Poetry is thus in its origin panegyrical. The first rude songs of all nations appear to be a sort of brief historical notices, in a strain of tumid hyperbole, of the exploits and possessions of a few pre-eminent individuals. They tell us how many battles such an one has fought, how many helmets he has cleft, how many breastplates he has pierced, how many widows he has made, how much land he has appropriated, how many houses he has demolished for other people, what a large one he has built for himself, how much gold he has stowed away in it, and how liberally and plentifully he pays, feeds, and intoxicates the divine and immortal bards, the sons of Jupiter, but for whose everlasting songs the names of heroes would perish.

This is the first stage of poetry before the invention of written letters. The numerical modulation is at once useful as a help to memory, and pleasant to the ears of uncultured men, who are easily caught by sound: and from the exceeding flexibility of the yet unformed language, the poet does no violence to his ideas in subjecting them to the fetters of number. The savage indeed lisps in numbers, and all rude and uncivilized people express themselves in the manner which we call poetical.

The scenery by which he is surrounded, and the superstitions which are the creed of his age, form the poet's mind. Rocks, mountains, seas, unsubdued forests, unnavigable rivers, surround him with forms of power and mystery, which ignorance and fear have peopled with spirits, under multifarious names of gods, goddesses, nymphs, genii, and daemons. Of all these personages marvellous tales are in existence: the nymphs are not indifferent to handsome young men, and the gentlemen-genii are much troubled and very troublesome with a propensity to be rude to pretty maidens: the bard therefore finds no difficulty in tracing the genealogy of his chief to any of the deities in his neighbourhood with whom the said chief may be most desirous of claiming relationship.

In this pursuit, as in all others, some of course will attain a very marked pre-eminence; and these will be held in high honour, like Demodocus in the *Odyssey*, and will be consequently inflated with boundless vanity, like Thamyris in the *Iliad*. Poets are as yet the only historians and chroniclers of their time, and the sole depositories of all the knowledge of their age; and though this knowledge is rather a crude congeries of traditional phantasies than a collection of useful truths, yet, such as it is, they have it to themselves. They are observing and thinking, while others are robbing and fighting: and though their object be nothing more than to secure a share of the spoil, yet they accomplish this end by intellectual, not by physical, power: their success excites emulation to the attainment of intellectual eminence: thus they sharpen their own wits and awaken those of others, at the same time that they gratify vanity and amuse curiosity. A skilful display of the little knowledge they have gains them credit for the possession of much more which they have not. Their familiarity with the secret history of gods and genii obtains for them, without much difficulty, the reputation of inspiration; thus they are not only historians but theologians, moralists, and legislators: delivering their oracles *ex cathedra*, and being indeed often themselves (as Orpheus and Amphion) regarded as portions and emanations of divinity: building cities with a song, and leading brutes with a symphony; which are only metaphors for the faculty of leading multitudes by the nose.

The golden age of poetry finds its materials in the age of iron. This age begins when poetry begins to be retrospective; when something like a more extended system of civil polity is established; when personal strength and courage avail less to the aggrandizing of their possessor and to the making and marring of kings and kingdoms, and are checked by organized bodies, social institutions, and hereditary successions. Men also live more in the light of truth and within the interchange of observation; and thus perceive that the agency of gods and genii is not so frequent among themselves as, to judge from the songs and legends of the past time, it was among their ancestors. From these two circumstances, really diminished personal power, and apparently diminished familiarity with gods and genii, they very easily and naturally deduce two conclusions: 1st, That men are degenerated, and 2nd, That they are less in favour with the gods. The people of the petty states and colonies, which have now acquired stability and form, which owed their origin and first prosperity to the talents and courage of a single chief, magnify their founder through the mists of distance and tradition, and perceive him achieving wonders with a god or goddess always at his elbow. They find his name and his exploits thus magnified and accompanied in their traditionary songs, which are their only memorials. All that is said of him is in this character. There is nothing to contradict it. The man and his exploits and his tutelary deities are mixed and blended in one invariable association. The marvellous too is very much like a snowball: it grows as it rolls downward, till the little nucleus of truth which began its descent from the summit is hidden in the accumulation of superinduced hyperbole.

When tradition, thus adorned and exaggerated, has surrounded the founders of families and states with so much adventitious power and magnificence, there is no praise which a living poet can, without fear of being kicked for clumsy flattery, address to a living chief, that will not still leave the impression that the latter is not so great a man as his ancestors. The man must in this case be praised through his ancestors. Their greatness must be established, and he must be shown to be their worthy descendant. All the people of a state are interested in the founder of their state. All states that have harmonized into a common form of society, are interested in their respective founders. All men are interested in their ancestors. All men love to look back into the days that are past. In these circumstances traditional national poetry is reconstructed and brought like chaos into order and form. The interest is more universal: understanding is enlarged: passion still has scope and play: character is still various and strong: nature is still unsubdued and existing in all her beauty and magnificence, and men are not yet excluded from her observation by the magnitude of cities or the daily confinement of civic life: poetry is more an art: it requires greater skill in numbers, greater command of language, more extensive and various knowledge, and greater comprehensiveness of mind. It still exists without rivals in any other department of literature; and even the arts, painting and sculpture certainly, and music probably, are comparatively rude and imperfect. The whole field of intellect is its own. It has no rivals in history, nor in philosophy, nor in science. It is cultivated by the greatest intellects of the age, and listened to by all the rest. This is the age of Homer, the golden age of poetry. Poetry has now attained its perfection: it has attained the point which it cannot pass: genius therefore seeks new forms for the treatment of the same subjects: hence the lyric poetry of Pindar and Alcaeus, and the tragic poetry of Aeschylus and Sophocles. The favour of kings, the honour of the Olympic crown, the applause of present multitudes, all that can feed vanity and stimulate rivalry, await the successful cultivator of this art, till its forms become exhausted, and new rivals arise around it in new fields of literature, which gradually acquire more influence as, with the progress of reason and civilization, facts become more interesting than fiction: indeed the maturity of poetry may be considered the infancy of history. The transition from Homer to Herodotus is scarcely more remarkable than that from Herodotus to Thucydides: in the gradual dereliction of fabulous incident and ornamented language, Herodotus is as much a poet in relation to Thucydides as Homer is in relation to Herodotus. The history of Herodotus is half a poem: it was written while the whole field of literature yet belonged to the Muses, and the nine books of which it was composed were therefore of right, as well as of courtesy, superinscribed with their nine names.

Speculations, too, and disputes, on the nature of man and of mind; on moral duties and on good and evil; on the animate and inanimate components of the visible world; begin to share attention with the eggs of Leda and the horns of Io, and to draw off from poetry a portion of its once undivided audience.

Then comes the silver age, or the poetry of civilized life. This poetry is of two kinds, imitative and original. The imitative consists in recasting, and giving an exquisite polish to, the poetry of the age of gold: of this Virgil is the most obvious and striking example. The original is chiefly comic, didactic, or satiric: as in Menander, Aristophanes, Horace, and Juvenal. The poetry of this age is characterized by an exquisite and fastidious selection of words, and a laboured and somewhat monotonous harmony of expression: but its monotony consists in this, that experience having exhausted all the varieties of modulation, the civilized poetry selects the most beautiful, and prefers the repetition of these to ranging through the variety of all. But the best expression being that into which the idea naturally falls, it requires the utmost labour and care so to reconcile the inflexibility of civilized language and the laboured polish of versification with the idea intended to be expressed, that sense may not appear to be sacrificed to sound. Hence numerous efforts and rare success.

This state of poetry is however a step towards its extinction. Feeling and passion are best painted in, and roused by, ornamental and figurative language; but the reason and the understanding are best addressed in the simplest and most unvarnished phrase. Pure reason and dispassionate truth would be perfectly ridiculous in verse, as we may judge by versifying one of Euclid's demonstrations. This will be found true of all dispassionate reasoning whatever, and all reasoning that requires comprehensive views and enlarged combinations. It is only the more tangible points of morality, those which command assent at once, those which have a mirror in every mind, and in which the severity of reason is warmed and rendered palatable by being mixed up with feeling and imagination, that are applicable even to what is called moral poetry: and as the sciences of morals and of mind advance towards perfection, as they become more enlarged and comprehensive in their views, as reason gains the ascendancy in them over imagination and feeling, poetry can no longer accompany them in their progress, but drops into the back ground, and leaves them to advance alone.

Thus the empire of thought is withdrawn from poetry, as the empire of facts had been before. In respect of the latter, the poet of the age of iron celebrates the achievements of his contemporaries; the poet of the age of gold celebrates the heroes of the age of iron; the poet of the age of silver re-casts the poems of the age of gold: we may here see how very slight a ray of historical truth is sufficient to dissipate all the illusions of poetry. We know no more of the men than of the gods of the *Iliad*; no more of Achilles than we do of Thetis; no more of Hector and Andromache than we do of Vulcan and Venus: these belong altogether to poetry; history has no share in them: but Virgil knew better than to write an epic about Caesar; he left him to Livy; and travelled out of the confines of truth and history into the old regions of poetry and fiction.

Good sense and elegant learning, conveyed in polished and somewhat monotonous verse, are the perfection of the original and imitative poetry of civilized life. Its range is limited, and when exhausted, nothing remains but the crambe repetita of common-place, which at length becomes thoroughly wearisome, even to the most indefatigable readers of the newest new nothings.

It is now evident that poetry must either cease to be cultivated, or strike into a new path. The poets of the age of gold have been imitated and repeated till no new imitation will attract notice: the limited range of ethical and didactic poetry is exhausted: the associations of daily life in an advanced state of society are

19

of very dry, methodical, unpoetical matters-of-fact: but there is always a multitude of listless idlers, yawning for amusement, and gaping for novelty: and the poet makes it his glory to be foremost among their purveyors.

Then comes the age of brass, which, by rejecting the polish and the learning of the age of silver, and taking a retrograde stride to the barbarisms and erude traditions of the age of iron, professes to return to nature and revive the age of gold. This is the second childhood of poetry. To the comprehensive energy of the Homeric Muse, which, by giving at once the grand outline of things, presented to the mind a vivid picture in one or two verses, inimitable alike in simplicity and magnificence, is substituted a verbose and minutely-detailed description of thoughts, passions, actions, persons, and things, in that loose rambling style of verse, which any one may write, stans pede in uno, at the rate of two hundred lines in an hour. To this age may be referred all the poets who flourished in the decline of the Roman Empire. The best specimen of it, though not the most generally known, is the Dionysiaca of Nonnus, which contains many passages of exceeding beauty in the midst of masses of amplification and repetition.

The iron age of classical poetry may be called the bardic; the golden, the Homeric; the silver, the Virgilian; and the brass, the Nonnic.

Modern poetry has also its four ages: but "it wears its rue with a difference."

To the age of brass in the ancient world succeeded the dark ages, in which the light of the Gospel began to spread over Europe, and in which, by a mysterious and inscrutable dispensation, the darkness thickened with the progress of the light. The tribes that overran the Roman Empire brought back the days of barbarism, but with this difference, that there were many books in the world, many places in which they were preserved, and occasionally some one by whom they were read, who indeed (if he escaped being burned *pour l'amour de Dieu,*) generally lived an object of mysterious fear, with the reputation of magician, alchymist, and astrologer. The emerging of the nations of Europe from this superinduced barbarism, and their settling into new forms of polity, was accompanied, as the first ages of Greece had been, with a wild spirit of adventure, which, co-operating with new manners and new superstitions, raised up a fresh crop of chimaeras, not less fruitful, though far less beautiful, than those of Greece. The semi- deification of women by the maxims of the age of chivalry, combining with these new fables, produced the romance of the middle ages. The founders of the new line of heroes took the place of the demi-gods of Grecian poetry. Charlemagne and his Paladins, Arthur and his knights of the round table, the heroes of the iron age of chivalrous poetry, were seen through the same magnifying mist of distance, and their exploits were celebrated with even more extravagant hyperbole. These legends, combined with the exaggerated love that pervades the songs of the troubadours, the reputation of magic that attached to learned men, the infant wonders of natural philosophy, the crazy fanaticism of the crusades, the power and privileges of the great feudal chiefs, and the holy mysteries of monks and nuns, formed a state of society in which no two laymen could meet without fighting, and in which the three staple ingredients of lover, prize-fighter, and fanatic, that composed the basis of the character of every true man, were mixed up and diversified, in different individuals and classes, with so many distinctive excellencies, and under such an infinite motley variety of costume, as gave the range of a most extensive and picturesque field to the two great constituents of poetry, love and battle.

From these ingredients of the iron age of modern poetry, dispersed in the rhymes of minstrels and the songs of the troubadours, arose the golden age, in which the scattered materials were harmonized and blended about the time of the revival of learning; but with this peculiar difference, that Greek and Roman literature pervaded all the poetry of the golden age of modern poetry, and hence resulted a heterogeneous compound

21

of all ages and nations in one picture; an infinite licence, which gave to the poet the free range of the whole field of imagination and memory. This was carried very far by Ariosto, but farthest of all by Shakespeare and his contemporaries, who used time and locality merely because they could not do without them, because every action must have its when and where: but they made no scruple of deposing a Roman Emperor by an Italian Count, and sending him off in the disguise of a French pilgrim to be shot with a blunderbuss by an English archer. This makes the old English drama very picturesque, at any rate, in the variety of costume, and very diversified in action and character; though it is a picture of nothing that ever was seen on earth except a Venetian carnival.

The greatest of English poets, Milton, may be said to stand alone between the ages of gold and silver, combining the excellencies of both; for with all the energy, and power, and freshness of the first, he united all the studied and elaborate magnificence of the second.

The silver age succeeded; beginning with Dryden, coming to perfection with Pope, and ending with Goldsmith, Collins, and Gray.

Cowper divested verse of its exquisite polish; he thought in metre, but paid more attention to his thoughts than his verse. It would be difficult to draw the boundary of prose and blank verse between his letters and his poetry.

The silver age was the reign of authority; but authority now began to be shaken, not only in poetry but in the whole sphere of its dominion. The contemporaries of Gray and Cowper were deep and elaborate thinkers. The subtle scepticism of Hume, the solemn irony of Gibbon, the daring paradoxes of Rousseau, and the biting ridicule of Voltaire, directed the energies of four extraordinary minds to shake every portion of the reign of authority. Enquity was roused, the activity of intellect was excited, and poetry came in for its share of the general result. The changes had been rung on lovely maid and sylvan shade, summer heat and green retreat, waving trees and sighing breeze, gentle swains and amorous pains, by versifiers who took them on trust, as meaning something very soft and tender, without much caring what: but with this general activity of intellect came a necessity for even poets to appear to know something of what they professed to talk of. Thomson and Cowper looked at the trees and hills which so many ingenious gentlemen had rhymed about so long without looking at them at all, and the effect of the operation on poetry was like the discovery of a new world. Painting shared the influence, and the principles of picturesque beauty were explored by adventurous essayists with indefatigable pertinacity. The success which attended these experiments, and the pleasure which resulted from them, had the usual effect of all new enthusiasms, that of turning the heads of a few unfortunate persons, the patriarchs of the age of brass, who, mistaking the prominent novelty for the all-important totality, seem to have ratiocinated much in the following manner: "Poetical genius is the finest of all things, and we feel that we have more of it than any one ever had. The way to bring it to perfection is to cultivate poetical impressions exclusively. Poetical impressions can be received only among natural scenes: for all that is artificial is anti-poetical. Society is artificial, therefore we will live out of society. The mountains are natural, therefore we will live in the mountains. There we shall be shining models of purity and virtue, passing the whole day in the innocent and amiable occupation of going up and down hill, receiving poetical impressions, and communicating them in immortal verse to admiring generations." To some such perversion of intellect we owe that egregious confraternity of rhymesters, known by the name of the Lake Poets; who certainly did receive and communicate to the world some of the most extraordinary poetical impressions that ever were heard of, and ripened into models of public virtue, too splendid to need illustration. They wrote verses on a new principle; saw rocks and rivers in a new light; and remaining studiously ignorant of history, society, and human nature, cultivated the phantasy only at the expence of the memory and the reason; and contrived, though they had retreated from the world for the express purpose of seeing nature as she was, to see her only as she was not, converting the land they lived in into a sort of fairy-land, which they peopled with mysticisms and chimaeras. This gave what is called a new tone to poetry, and conjured up a herd of desperate imitators, who have brought the age of brass prematurely to its dotage.

The descriptive poetry of the present day has been called by its cultivators a return to nature. Nothing is more impertinent than this pretension. Poetry cannot travel out of the regions of its birth, the uncultivated lands of semi-civilized men. Mr. Wordsworth, the great leader of the returners to nature, cannot describe a scene under his own eyes without putting into it the shadow of a Danish boy or the living ghost of Lucy Gray, or some similar phantastical parturition of the moods of his own mind.

In the origin and perfection of poetry, all the associations of life were composed of poetical materials. With us it is decidedly the reverse. We know too that there are no Dryads in Hyde-park nor Naiads in the Regent's-canal. But barbaric manners and supernatural interventions are essential to poetry. Either in the scene, or in the time, or in both, it must be remote from our ordinary perceptions. While the historian and the philosopher are advancing in, and accelerating, the progress of knowledge, the poet is wallowing in the rubbish of departed ignorance, and raking up the ashes of dead savages to find gewgaws and rattles for the grown babies of the age. Mr. Scott digs up the poachers and cattle-stealers of the ancient border. Lord Byron cruizes for thieves and pirates on the shores of the Morea and among the Greek Islands. Mr. Southey wades through ponderous volumes of travels and old chronicles, from which he carefully selects all that is false, useless, and absurd, as being essentially poetical; and when he has a commonplace book full of monstrosities, strings them into an epic. Mr. Wordsworth picks up village legends from old women and sextons; and Mr. Coleridge, to the valuable information acquired from similar sources, superadds the dreams of crazy theologians and the mysticisms of German metaphysics, and favours the world with visions in verse, in which the quadruple elements of sexton, old woman, Jeremy Taylor, and Emanuel Kant, are harmonized into a delicious poetical compound. Mr. Moore presents us with a Persian, and Mr. Campbell with a Pennsylvanian tale, both formed on the same principle as Mr. Southey's epics, by extracting from a perfunctory and desultory perusal of a collection of voyages and travels, all that useful investigation would not seek for and that common sense would reject.

These disjointed relics of tradition and fragments of second-hand observation, being woven into a tissue of verse, constructed on what Mr. Coleridge calls a new principle (that is, no principle at all), compose a modern-antique compound of frippery and barbarism, in which the puling sentimentality of the present time is grafted on the misrepresented ruggedness of the past into a heterogeneous congeries of unamalgamating manners, sufficient to impose on the common readers of poetry, over whose understandings the poet of this class possesses that commanding advantage, which, in all circumstances and conditions of life, a man who knows something, however little, always possesses over one who knows nothing.

A poet in our times is a semi-barbarian in a civilized community. He lives in the days that are past. His ideas, thoughts, feelings, associations, are all with barbarous manners, obsolete customs, and exploded superstitions. The march of his intellect is like that of a crab, backward. The brighter the light diffused around him by the progress of reason, the thicket is the darkness of antiquated barbarism, in which he buries himself like a mole, to throw up the barren hillocks of his Cimmerian labours. The philosophic mental tranquillity which looks round with an equal eye on all external things, collects a store of ideas, discriminates their relative value, assigns to all their proper place, and from the materials of useful knowledge thus collected, appreciated, and arranged, forms new combinations that impress the stamp of their power and utility on the real business of life, is diametrically the reverse of that frame of mind which poetry inspires, or from which poetry can emanate. The highest inspirations of poetry are resolvable into three ingredients: the rant of unregulated passion, the whining of exaggerated feeling, and the cant of factitious sentiment: and can therefore serve only to ripen a splendid lunatic like Alexander, a puling driveller like Werter, or a morbid dreamer like Wordsworth. It can never make a philosopher, nor a statesman, nor in any class of life an useful or rational man. It cannot claim the slightest share in any one of the comforts and utilities of life of which we have witnessed so many and so rapid advances. But though not useful, it may be said it is highly ornamental, and deserves to be cultivated for the pleasure it yields. Even if this be granted, it does not follow that a writer of poetry in the present state of society is not a waster of his own time, and a robber of that of others. Poetry is not one of those arts which, like painting, require repetition and multiplication, in order to be diffused among society. There are more good poems already existing than are sufficient to employ that portion of life which any mere reader and recipient of poetical impressions should devote to them, and these having been produced in poetical times, are far superior in all the characteristics of poetry to the artificial reconstructions of a few morbid ascetics in unpoetical times. To read the promiscuous rubbish of the present time to the exclusion of the select treasures of the past, is to substitute the worse for the better variety of the same mode of enjoyment.

But in whatever degree poetry is cultivated, it must necessarily be to the neglect of some branch of useful study: and it is a lamentable spectacle to see minds, capable of better things, running to seed in the specious indolence of these empty aimless mockeries of intellectual exertion. Poetry was the mental rattle that awakened the attention of intellect in the infancy of civil society: but for the maturity of mind to make a serious business of the playthings of its childhood, is as absurd as for a full-grown man to rub his gums with coral, and cry to be charmed to sleep by the jingle of silver bells.

As to that small portion of our contemporary poetry, which is neither descriptive, nor narrative, nor dramatic, and which, for want of a better name, may be called ethical, the most distinguished portion of it, consisting merely of querulous, egotistical rhapsodies, to express the writer's high dissatisfaction with the world and every thing in it, serves only to confirm what has been said of the semibarbarous character of poets, who from singing dithyrambics and "Io Triumphe," while society was savage, grow rabid, and out of their element, as it becomes polished and enlightened.

Now when we consider that it is not the thinking and studious, and scientific and philosophical part of the community, not to those whose minds are bent on the pursuit and promotion of permanently useful ends and aims, that poets must address their minstrelsy, but to that much larger portion of the reading public, whose minds are not awakened to the desire of valuable knowledge, and who are indifferent to any thing beyond being charmed, moved, excited, affected, and exalted: charmed by harmony, moved by sentiment, excited by passion, affected by pathos, and exalted by sublimity: harmony, which is language on the rack of Procrustes; sentiment, which is canting egotism in the mask of refined feeling; passion, which is the commotion of a weak and selfish mind; pathos, which is the whining of an unmanly spirit; and sublimity, which is the inflation of an empty head: when we consider that the great and permanent interests of human society become more and more the main spring of intellectual pursuit; that in proportion as they become so, the subordinacy of the ornamental to the useful will be more and more seen and acknowledged; and that therefore the progress of useful art and science, and of moral and political knowledge, will continue more and more to withdraw attention from frivolous and unconducive, to solid and conducive studies:

that therefore the poetical audience will not only continually diminish in the proportion of its number to that of the rest of the reading public, but will also sink lower and lower in the comparison of intellectual acquirement: when we consider that the poet must still please his audience, and must therefore continue to sink to their level, while the rest of the community is rising above it: we may easily conceive that the day is not distant, when the degraded state of every species of poetry will be as generally recognized as that of dramatic poetry has long been: and this not from any decrease either of intellectual power, or intellectual acquisition, but because intellectual power and intellectual acquisition have turned themselves into other and better channels, and have abandoned the cultivation and the fate of poetry to the degenerate fry of modern rhymesters, and their olympic judges, the magazine critics, who continue to debate and promulgate oracles about poetry, as if it were still what it was in the Homeric age, the all-in-all of intellectual progression, and as if there were no such things in existence as mathematicians, astronomers, chemists, moralists, metaphysicians, historians, politicians, and political economists, who have built into the upper air of intelligence a pyramid, from the summit of which they see the modern Parnassus far beneath them, and, knowing how small a place it occupies in the comprehensiveness of their prospect, smile at the little ambition and the circumscribed perceptions with which the drivellers and mountebanks upon it are contending for the poetical palm and the critical chair. [3]

NOTES

[1   T. Petronius Arbiter,*Satyricon*, II. "They who are fed on these things can no more be wise than those who dwell in the kitchen can be fragrant."]

2   See the *Odyssey,* passim: and Thucydides, I. 5.

[3   On the 21st of March, 1821, Shelley wrote to Peacock:---'I dispatch by this post the first part of an essay, intended to consist of three parts, which I design for an antidote to your *Four Ages of Poetry.* You will see that I have taken a more general view of what poetry is than you have, and will perhaps agree with several of my positions, without considering your own touched.' Peacock annotates:---'The *Four Ages of Poetry* here alluded to was published in Ollier's *Literary Miscellany.* Shelley wrote the Defence of Poetry as an answer to it; and as he wrote it, it contained many allusions to the article and its author, such as "If I know the knight by the device of his shield, I have only to inscribe Cassandra, Antigone, or Alcestis on mine to blunt the point of his spear;" taking one instance of a favourite character from each of the the three great Greek tragedians. All these allusions were struck out by Mr. John Hunt when he prepared the paper for publication in the *Liberal.* The demise of that periodical prevented the publication, and Mrs. Shelley subsequently printed it from Mr. Hunt's *rifacciamento,* as she received it. The paper as it now stands is a defence without an attack. Shelley intended this paper to be in three parts, but the other two were not written.' quoted from H.F.B. Brett-Smith & C.E. Jones, vol. viii, p. 500]

RECOLLECTIONS OF CHILDHOOD

The Abbey House

1837

I PASSED many of my earliest days in a country town, on whose immediate outskirts stood an ancient mansion, bearing the name of the Abbey House. [1] This mansion has long since vanished from the face of the earth; but many of my pleasantest youthful recollections are associated with it, and in my mind's eye I can still see it as it stood, with its amiable, simple-mannered, old English inhabitants.

The house derived its name from standing near, though not actually on, the site of one of those rich old abbeys, whose demesnes the pure devotion of Henry the Eighth transferred from their former occupants (who foolishly imagined they had a right to them, though they lacked the might which is its essence,) to the members of his convenient parliamentary chorus, who helped him run down his Scotch octave of wives. Of the abbey itself a very small portion remained: a gateway, and a piece of a wall which formed part of the enclosure of an orchard, wherein a curious series of fish-ponds, connected by sluices, was fed from a contiguous stream with a perpetual circulation of fresh water,---a sort of piscatorial panopticon, where all approved varieties of fresh-water fish had been classified, each in its own pond, and kept in good order, clean and fat, for the mortification of the flesh of the monastic brotherhood on fast-days.

The road which led to the Abbey House terminated as a carriage-road with the house itself. Beyond it, a footpath over meadows conducted across a ferry to a village about a mile distant. A large clump of old walnut-trees stood on the opposite side of the road to a pair of massy iron gates, which gave entrance to a circular gravel road, encompassing a large smooth lawn, with a sun-dial in the centre, and bordered on both sides with tall thick evergreens and flowering shrubs, interspersed in the seasons with hollyhocks, sunflowers, and other gigantic blossoms, such as are splendid in distance. Within, immediately opposite the gates, a broad flight of stone steps led to a ponderous portal, and to a large antique hall, laid with a chequered pavement of black and white marble. On the left side of the entrance was the porter's chair, consisting of a cushioned seat, occupying the depth of a capacious recess resembling a niche for a full-sized statue, a well-stuffed body of black leather glittering with gold-headed nails. On the right of this hall was the great staircase; on the left, a passage to a wing appropriated to the domestics.

Facing the portal, a door opened into an inner hall, in the centre of which was a billiard table. On the right of this hall was a library; on the left a parlour, which was the common sitting-room; and facing the middle door was a glazed door, opening on the broad flight of stone steps which led into the gardens.

The gardens were in the old style: a large square lawn occupied an ample space in the centre, separated by broad walks from belts of trees and shrubs on each side; and in front were two advancing groves, with a long wide vista between them, looking to the open country, from which the grounds were separated by a terraced wall over a deep sunken dyke. One of the groves we called the green grove, and the other the dark grove. The first had a pleasant glade, with sloping banks covered with flowery turf; the other was a mass of trees, too closely canopied with foliage for grass to grow beneath them.

The family [2] consisted of a gentleman and his wife, with two daughters and a son. The eldest daughter was on the confines of womanhood, the youngest was little more than a child; the son was between them. I do not know his exact age, but I was seven or eight, and he was two or three years more.

The family lived, from taste, in a very retired manner; but to the few whom they received they were eminently hospitable. I was perhaps the foremost among these few; for Charles, who was my schoolfellow, was never happy in our holidays unless I was with him. A frequent guest was an elderly male relation, much respected by the family,---but no favourite of Charles, over whom he was disposed to assume greater authority than Charles was willing to acknowledge.

The mother and daughter had all the solid qualities which were considered female virtues in the dark ages. Our enlightened age has, wisely no doubt, discarded many of them, and substituted show for solidity. The dark ages preferred the natural blossom, and the fruit that follows it; the enlightened age prefers the artificial double-blossom, which falls and leaves nothing. But the double blossom is brilliant while it lasts; and where there is so much light, there ought to be something to glitter in it.

These ladies had the faculty of staying at home; and this was a principal among the antique faculties that upheld the rural mansions of the middling gentry. Ask Brighton, Cheltenham, *et id genus omne,* [3] what has become of that faculty. And ask the ploughshare what has become of the rural mansions.

They never, I think, went out of their own grounds but to church, or to take their regular daily airing in the old family-carriage. The young lady was an adept at preserving: she had one room, in a corner of the hall, between the front and the great staircase, entirely surrounded with shelves in compartments, stowed with classified sweetmeats, jellies, and preserved fruits, the work of her own sweet hands. These wee distinguished ornaments of the supper-table; for the family dined early, and maintained the old fashion of supper. A child would not easily forget the bountiful and beautiful array of fruits, natural and preserved, and the ample variety of preparations of milk, cream, and custard, by which they were accompanied. The supper-table had matter for all tastes. I remember what was most to mine.

The young lady performed on the harpsichord. Over what a gulph of time this name alone looks back! What a stride from that harpsichord to one of Broadwood's last grand-pianos! And yet with what pleasure, as I stood by the corner of the instrument, I listened to it, or rather to her! I would give much to know that the worldly lot of this gentle and amiable creature had been a happy one. She often gently remonstrated with me for putting her harpsichord out of tune by playing the bells upon it; but I was never in a serious scrape with her except once. I had insisted on taking from the nursery-maid the handle of the little girl's garden-carriage, with which I set off at full speed; and had not run many yards before I overturned the carriage, and rolled out the little girl. The child cried like Alice Fell, and would not be pacified. Luckily she ran to her sister, who let me off with an admonition, and the exaction of a promise never to meddle again with the child's carriage.

Charles was fond of romances. The *Mysteries of Udolpho*, [4] and all the ghost and goblin stories of the day, were his familiar reading. I cared little about them at the time; but he amused me by narrating their grimmest passages. He was very anxious that the Abbey House should be haunted; but it had no strange sights or sounds, and no plausible tradition to hang a ghost on. I had very nearly accommodated him with what he wanted.

The garden-front of the house was covered with jasmine, and it was a pure delight to stand in the summer twilight on the top of the stone steps inhaling the fragrance of the multitudinous blossoms. One evening, as I was standing on these steps alone, I saw something like the white head-dress of a tall figure advance from the right-hand grove,---the dark grove, as we called it,--- and, after a brief interval, recede. This, at any rate, looked awful. Presently it appeared again, and again vanished. On which I jumped to my conclusion, and flew into the parlour with the announcement that there was a ghost in the dark grove. The whole family sallied forth to see the phenomenon. The appearances and disappearances continued. All conjectured what it could be, but none could divine. In a minute or two all the servants were in the hall. They all tried their skill, and all were equally unable to solve the riddle. At last, the master of the house leading the way, we marched in a body to the spot, and unravelled the mystery. It was a large bunch of flowers on top of a tall lily, waving in the wind at the edge of the grove, and disappearing at intervals behind the stem of a tree. My ghost, and the compact phalanx in which we sallied against it, were long the subject of merriment. It was a cruel disappointment to Charles, who was obliged to abandon all hopes of having the house haunted.

One day Charles was in disgrace with his elderly relation, who had exerted sufficient authority to make him captive in his chamber. He was prohibited from seeing anyone but me; and, of course, a most urgent messenger was sent to me express. I found him in his chamber, sitting by the fire, with a pile of ghostly tales, and an accumulation of lead, which he was casting into dumps in a mould. Dumps, the inexperienced reader must know, are flat circles of lead,---a sort of petty quoits,---with which schoolboys amused themselves half a century ago, and perhaps do so still, unless the march of mind has marched off with such vanities. No doubt, in the "astounding progress of intellect," the time will arrive when boys will play at philosophers instead of playing at soldiers,---will fight with wooden arguments instead of wooden swords,---and pitch leaden syllogisms instead of leaden dumps. Charles was before the dawn of this new light. He had cast several hundred dumps, and was still at work. The quibble did not occur to me at the time; but, in after years, I never heard of a man in the dumps without thinking of my schoolfellow. His position was sufficiently melancholy. His chamber was at the end of a long corridor. He was determined not to make any submission, and his captivity was likely to last till the end of his holidays. Ghost-stories, and lead for dumps, were his stores and provisions for standing the siege of *ennui*. I think, with the aid of his sister, I had some share in making his peace; but, such is the association of ideas, that, when I first read in Lord Byron's *Don Juan*,

'I pass my evenings in my long galleries solely,
And that's the reason I'm so melancholy,"

the lines immediately conjured up the image of poor Charles in the midst of his dumps and spectres at the end of his own long gallery.

NOTES

1   "The Abbey House appeared in the February number of *Bentley's Miscellany* for 1837 (Vol. I. pp.187-90), under a heading which suggests that Peacock was then contemplating a series of early reminiscences: 'RECOLLECTIONS OF CHILDHOOD. | BY THE AUTHOR OF HEADLONG HALL. | [short rule] | THE ABBEY HOUSE.'" from H.F.B. Brett-Smith & C.E. Jones, vol viii, p. 495.

2   The family in the Abbey House were surnamed Barwell: "The Barwell family had strong associations with East India House."---note 14, on p. 291 in *Thomas Love Peacock* by Felix Felton, London, George Allen & Unwin (1972).

3   and all of that kind (Latin)

4   *The Mysteries of Udolpho*, by Ann Radcliffe (1764-1823), was first printed in 1794. See Chapter VI of *Northanger Abbey* by Jane Austen (published posthumously in 1818), for Catherine Morland's similar literary tastes.

THE LAST DAY OF WINDSOR FOREST

1862

MANY of my younger, and some of my maturer years, were passed on the borders of Windsor Forest. I was early given to long walks and rural explorations, and there was scarcely a spot of the Park or the Forest, with which I was not intimately acquainted. There were two very different scenes, to which I was especially attached: Virginia Water, and a dell near Winkfield plain.

The bank of Virginia Water, on which the public enter from the Wheatsheaf Inn, is bordered, between the cascade to the left and the iron gates to the right, by groves of trees, which, with the exception of a few old ones near the water, have grown up within my memory. They were planted by George the Third, [1] and the entire space was called the King's Plantation. Perhaps they were more beautiful in an earlier age than they are now: or I may so think and feel, through the general preference of the past to the present, which seems inseparable from old age. In my first acquaintance with the place, and for some years subsequently, sitting in the large upper room of the Inn, I could look on the cascade and the expanse of the lake, which have long been masked by trees.

Virginia Water was always open to the public, through the Wheatsheaf Inn, except during the Regency and Reign of George the Fourth, who not only shut up the grounds, but enclosed them, where they were open to a road, with higher fences than even the outside passengers of stage-coaches could look over, that he might be invisible in his punt, while fishing on the lake. William the Fourth lowered the fences, and re-opened the old access.

While George the Third was king, Virginia Water was a very solitary place. I have been there day after day, without seeing another visitor. Now it has many visitors. It is a source of great enjoyment to many, though no longer suitable to *Les RÆveries d'un Promeneur Solitaire.*

A still more solitary spot, which had especial charms for me, was the deep forest dell already mentioned, on the borders of Winkfield Plain. This dell, I think, had the name of the Bourne, but I always called it the Dingle. In the bottom was a watercourse, which was a stream only in times of continuous rain. Old trees clothed it on both sides to the summit, and it was a favourite resort of deer. I was a witness of their banishment from their forest-haunts. The dell itself remained some time unchanged: but I have not seen it since 1815, when I frequently visited it in company with Shelley, during his residence at Bishopgate, on the eastern side of the Park. I do not know what changes it may have since undergone. Not much, perhaps, being now a portion of the Park. But many portions of the Park and its vicinity, as well as of the immediate neighbourhood of Windsor, which were then open to the public, have ceased to be so, and such may be the case with this. I have never ventured to acertain the point. In all the portions of the old forest, which were distributed in private allotments, I know what to expect. I shrink from the ghosts of my old associations in scenery, and never, if I can help it, revisit an enclosed locality, with which I have been familiar in its openness.

Wordsworth would not visit Yarrow, because he feared to disappoint his imagination:

> Be Yarrow stream unseen, unknown!
> It must, or we shall rue it:
> We have a vision of our own,
> Ah! why should we undo it?

The treasured dreams of times long past,
We'll keep them, winsome Marrow!
For then we're there, although 'tis fair,
'Twill be another Yarrow. [2]

Yet, when he afterwards visited it, though it was not what he had dreamed, he still found it beautiful, and rejoiced in having seen it:

The vapours linger round the heights:
They melt, and soon must vanish:
One hour is theirs, nor more is mine:
Sad thought which I would banish,
But that I know, where'er I go,
Thy genuine image Yarrow!
Will dwell with me, to heighten joy,
And cheer my mind in sorrow. [3]

He found compensation in the reality, for the difference of the imagined scene: but there is no such compensation for the disappointments of memory: and when---in the place of scenes of youth, where we have wandered under antique trees, through groves and glades, through bushes and underwood, among fern, and foxglove, and bounding deer; where, perhaps, every "minutest circumstance of place"[4] has been not only "as a friend" in itself, but has recalled some association of early friendship, or youthful love---we can only pass between high fences along dusty roads, I think it best to avoid the sight of the reality, and to make the best of cherishing at a distance

The memory of what has been,
And never more will be. [5]

I do not express, or imply, any opinion on the general utility of enclosures. For the most part, they illustrate the scriptural maxim: "To him that hath much, much shall be given; and from him that hath little, shall be taken away even the little he hath."[6] They are, like most events in this world, "Good to some, bad to others, and indifferent to the majority." They are good to the landowner, who gets an addition to his land: they are bad to the poor parishioner, who loses his rights of common: they are bad to the lover of rural walks, for whom footpaths are annihilated: they are bad to those, fro whom the scenes of their youth are blotted from the face of the world. These last are of no account in ledger balances, which profess to demonstrate that the loss of the poor is more than counterbalanced by the gain of the rich; that the aggregate gain is the gain of the community; and that all matters of taste and feeling are fitly represented by a cypher. So be it.

George the Fourth's exclusions and high fences had not, however, effectually secured to him the secrecy he desired. On an eminence outside of the royal grounds, stood, and still stands, in the midst of a pine-grove, a tower, which from its form was commonly called the Clock-case. This tower, and the land round it, had been sold for a small sum, as a lot in a sale of Crown Lands. The tower was in two or three stories, and was inhabited by a poor family, who had a telescope, supplied, most probably, by the new proprietor, on the platform of the roof, which rose high above the trees, and commanded an extensive view of the lake. This tower and its grounds became a place of great resort for pic-nic parties, and visitors of all kinds, who kept up a perpetual succession at the telescope, while the Royal Angler and his fair companion were fishing. This became an intolerable nuisance to the would-be-recluse. He set on foot a negociation for re-purchasing the Clock-case. The sum demanded was many times the multiple of the purchase-money. The demand was for some time resisted, but the proprietor was inflexible. The sum required was paid, the property reverted to the Crown, and the public were shut out from the Clock-case and its territory. When William the Fourth succeeded, this story was told to him, and he said: "A good place for a view, is it? I will put an old couple into it, and give them a telescope:" which was done without loss of time. I saw and conversed with this old couple, and looked through their telescope.

About the same time, William the Fourth was sitting one Sunday evening in a window of Windsor Castle, when the terrace was thronged with people.

A heavy rain came on, and the people ran in all directions. He said to one near him: "This is the strangest thing I ever saw: so many English people, without an umbrella among them." He was told that, by order of his late Majesty, umbrellas were prohibited on the terrace. "Then," he said, "let the prohibition be immediately withdrawn."

In the early days of his reign, he was fond of walking about, not only in Windsor, but in London. It pleased him to be among the people. In one of his walks, he noticed, in Windsor Little Park, a board with an inscription, by which all persons were "ordered" to keep the footpath. He desired that "requested" might be substituted. He was told that "requested" would not be attended to. He said: "If they will not attend to 'requested' that is their affair: I will not have 'ordered.'"

A most good-natured, kind-hearted gentleman was William the Fourth: but to record the many instances of good feeling in his sayings and doings, which came within my knowledge, would be foreign to the purpose of the present paper.

The Act for the enclosure of Windsor Forest contained the following clause:---

WINDSOR FOREST.
53rd George III. Cap. 158.

LXIV.---And be it further enacted, That from and after the first day of July one thousand eight hundred and fourteen, all and singular the Lands, Tenements and Heridaments within the said respective Parishes and Liberties (save and except such Parts thereof respectively as are now or shall or may become vested in His Majesty, or any Person or Persons in Trust for Him by virtue hereof) shall be, and the same is and are hereby disafforested to all Intents and Purposes whatsoever; and that from thenceforth no Person or Persons shall be questioned or liable to any Pain, Penalty or Punishment for hunting, coursing, killing, destroying or taking any Deer whatsoever within the same, save and except within such Part or Parts thereof (if any) as shall be enclosed within Pales and kept for a Park or Parks by the Owners, Lesees, or Tenants thereof.

There can be little doubt, that the exception in favour of the Crown was intended to apply to all the provisions of the lause: but it was held by Counsel learned in law, that it applied to the first half only, and that, after the specified day, it was lawful to kill deer in any portion of the old forest, not enclosed with pales, whether such portion had, or had not, been vested in the Crown. The Crown allotment had been left as it was.   Armed with this opinion, a farmer of Water Oakley, whose real name I have forgotten in his assumed name, calling himself Robin Hood, and taking with him two of his men, whom he called Scarlet and Little John, sallied forth daily into the forest to kill the king's deer, and returned home every evening, loaded with spoil.

Lord Harcourt, who was then Deputy Ranger of the Forest, and discharged all the duties of superintendence (for the Ranger, who was a Royal Highness, of course did nothing), went forth also, as the representative of Majesty, to put down these audacious trespassers. In my forest rambles, I was a witness to some of their altercations: Lord Harcourt threatening to ruin Robin Hood by process in the Court of Exchequer; Robin Hood setting him at defiance, flourishing the Act of Parliament, and saying: "My Lord, if you don't know how to make Acts of Parliament, I'll teach you."

One day, I was walking towards the Dingle, when I met a man with a gun, who asked me, if I had seen Robin Hood? I said, I had just seen him at a little distance, in discussion with Lord Harcourt, who was on horseback, Robin Hood being on foot. He asked me to point out the direction, which I did; and in return I asked him, Who he might be? He told me, he was Scarlet. He was a pleasant-looking man, and seemed as merry as his original: like one in high enjoyment of sport.

This went on some time. The law was not brought to bear on Robin Hood, and it was finally determined to settle the matter, by driving the deer out of the forest into the Park. Two regiments of cavalry were employed for this purpose, which was kept as secret as possibe, for a concourse of people would have been a serious impediment to the operation. I received intelligence of it from a friend at court, who pointed out to me a good position, from which to view the close of the proceedings.

My position was on rising ground, covered with trees, and overlooking an extensive glade. The park was on my left hand: the main part of the forest on the right and before me. A wide extent of the park paling had been removed, and rope fencing had been carried to a great length, at oblique angles from the opening. It was a clear calm sunny day, and for a time there was a profound silence. This was first broken by the faint sound of bugles, answering each other's signals from remote points in the distance: drawing nearer by degrees, and groing progressively loud. The came two or three straggling deer, bounding from the trees, and flying through the opening of the park pales. Then came greater numbers, and ultimately congregated herds: the beatings of their multitudinous feet mingled with the trampling of the yet unseen horses, and the full sounds of the bugles. Last appeared the cavalry, issuing from the woods, and ranging themselves in a semi-circle, from horn to horn of the rope fencing. The open space was filled with deer, terrified by the chace, confused by their own numbers, and rushing in all directions: the greater part through the park opening: many trying to leap the rope fencing, in which a few were hurt; and one or two succeeded: escaping to their old haunts, most probably to furnish Robin Hood with his last venison feast. By degrees, the mass grew thinner: at last, all had disappeared: the rope fencing shut up the park for the night: the cavalry rode off towards Windsor: and all again was silent.

This was, without any exception, the most beautiful sight I ever witnessed: but I saw it with deep regret: for, with the expulsion of the deer, the life of the old scenes was gone, and I have always looked back on that day, as the last day of Windsor Forest. [7]

FOOTNOTES

[1 "I am not a fair judge of George the Third. I passed many of my earliest years in the neighbourhood of Windsor, where he was certainly popular. He lived much in public, attending every day at Ascot and Egham races, riding on horseback in the park and forest. There was not a trace, then, of the system of exclusion which has destroyed to me all the charm of the neighbourhood. Subsequently, too, I liked to see him at the theatre. He went week after week to Covent Garden, and there was something very genial in his hearty enjoyment of Comedy. You see I have pleasantassociations with him, which have nothing to do with politics, but have their influence in judgement of character." from a letter to Thomas L'Estrange, 26 July, 1861, replying to L'Estrange's comment that since George the Third's "frugality sprung from avarice and is hostility to the Whigs from his love of arbitrary power I cannot regard him as a patriot . . .".]

2   Yarrow Unvisited

3   Yarrow Visited

4   But thou hast viewed

These scenes, like one who passes through a land,
Where his heart is not. I, my friend, long time
Had sojourned there; and I am one who form
With each minutest circumstance of place
Acquaintance, and the unfrequented field,
Where many a day I walk in solitude,
Is as a friend to me.

Southey's Epistle to Amos Cottle, prefixed to the latter's
Icelandic Poetry. It is strange, that this Epistle was not included in
Southey's collected works. It is one of the best of his minor poems,
and would alone suffice top show, that he had "looked on nature
with a poet's eye."

5   Wordsworth.

[6   *Matt.* xiii, 12]

[7   In H.F.B. Brett-Smith & C.E. Jones (vol. viii, p. 504) it is
noted that *The Last Day of Windsor Forest* was first published by
Richard Garner in the September number of the *National Review*
for 1887, with a prefatory note wherein Garner observed that "It
was in all probability intended for *Fraser's Magazine*, but never
appeared there, nor, so far as can be discovered, elsewhere. The
probable date of composition is about 1862."

See also Peacock's letter to E.T. Hookham of 17 May, 1809,
from Chertsey, wherein Peacock writes: "Let me just recall to
your mind the King's Plantation, the cultivated corner by the
chevaux-de-frize gates, Chapel Wood, the seat under the oak, the
old fisherman's punt, the magnificent beech, the £12,000 bridge,
the Belvedere, the laurel walk, the iron gate under the arch, my
favourite pine grove on the bank of the water, the Cascade, &c, &c,
&c."]

PROSPECTUS:
CLASSICAL EDUCATION

THE PRINCIPAL object of education is to communicate to the youthful mind that love of mental and moral improvement, which will continue to act with a steady and permanent impression when no longer directed by the hand of the preceptor. That this disposition is most effectively promoted by an intimate acquaintance with the poets, philosophers, and historians of antiquity appears to be generally acknowledged, though the total neglect of classical studies among the young men of the present age, who, in the language of the time have finished their education, seems to shew that in the method usually employed to introduce them to an acquaintance with these inimitable models of eloquence there is some inherent and radical defect.

In fact it too frequently happens that the instructors of youth aim only at communicating the knowledge of the words and rules of a language, without exciting the taste of the student to penetrate into the beauties of the authors who have written in it: and instead of leading him forward by an easy and pleasant progress, involve him in the first instance in studies so dry, disgusting, and repulsive that the first ideas he associates with classical literature are those of weariness, pain, and privation.

The youthful mind should be taught from the beginning to take pleasure in the acquisition of knowledge, and to pursue it for its own sake: when this object has not been accomplished, the end of education has not been answered.

The child who learns his lessons under the dread of punishment, or the hope of reward, may proceed with rapidity through the common routine of academical education, but when these motives cease to operate, the effects they have produced will terminate. The pupil who is made to feel the value of knowledge, and to pursue it for its intrinsic advantages and pleasures, is alone likely to become an accomplished and useful member of society.

The mind must be excited and awakened before it can be cultivated to advantage. On this account it was the opinion of the ancients that the first years of youth should be devoted to poetry. But it is not enough for this purpose to discipline a reluctant child with the minutiae of syntax and prosody: he must be led by the conviction of future gratification to proceed with diligence through these toilsome acquisitions, as the peasant must be to conceive a prospect of harvest before he can be stimulated to the labour of turning the soil.

The harmonious language and delightful poetry of Italy are admirably adapted to form the taste of youth, and must be regarded as an indispensable requirement of elegant education.

Those who have been educated in large cities are seldom persons of superior taste: to the acquisition of which an early acquaintance with the beauties of nature is indispensable. The youth who, unacquainted with the country, reads in a populous city the beautiful descriptions of Homer and Virgil, derives no pleasure from the language to which his fancy yields no corresponding images: but he who under kind and skilful superintendence, amidst the wild beauties of nature, associates the ideas of the great poets with the living landscapes around him, derives from the pleasure thus experienced an ardent love of letters which accomplishes at once the great objects of education, and of which the salutary effects will be felt to the latest period of life.

This mode of education, requiring more art and attention than the common mode of instruction, can only be properly pursued amongst a limited number of pupils, not so small as to exclude emulation, nor so numerous as to prevent the most sedulous attention to any individual of the establishment.

With these ideas, the writer of the prospectus proposes to

receive eight pupils, in a beautiful retirement in the county of Westmoreland, at 100 *Gs.* per annum. They will be educated in the religion of the established church, and the same attention will be paid to their health and morals as to the improvement of their minds.—

The principal objects of study will be the Greek, Latin, Italian and French languages; an intimate knowledge of the language and literature of England generally too much neglected in the education of youth—poetry–history–and mental and moral philosophy.

For further particulars, and unexceptionable testimonials as to ability and character, apply to......

www.ingramcontent.com/pod-product-compliance
Lightning Source LLC
Chambersburg PA
CBHW030910260626
47169CB00008B/2785